The Intimate Alphabet

The Intimate Alphabet

poems
by
Kathleen McHale

CORMORANT BOOKS

Copyright © Kathleen McHale, 1993

Published with the assistance of the Canada Council, the Ontario Arts Council, and the Government of Ontario through the Ministry of Culture and Communications.

Front cover art *Jack-in-the-Pulpit No. IV*, Alfred Stieglitz Collection, Bequest of Georgia O'Keeffe, © 1992 National Gallery of Art, Washington, 1930, oil on canvas, 1.016 x .762 (40 x 30).

Cover design by Artcetera Graphics, Dunvegan, Ontario.

Published by
    Cormorant Books Inc.
    RR 1
    Dunvegan, Ontario
    Canada K0C 1J0

Printed and bound in Canada

Canadian Cataloguing in Publication Data
    McHale, Kathleen, 1953-
        The intimate alphabet

    ISBN 0-920953-49-2

        1. O'Keeffe, Georgia, 1887-1986--Poetry. 2. Stieglitz, Alfred, 1864-1946--Poetry. I. Title.

    PS8575.H35168 1993   C811'.54   C93-090039-1
    PR9199.3.M34168 1993

*A
Gilles*

ABSTRACT

The Intimate Alphabet

Georgia O'Keeffe was a major force in twentieth-century American painting. She died in 1986 at the age of ninety-eight. Alfred Stieglitz, born in Germany, has been called the 'father of modern photography'. He supported many artists and introduced them to the North American art milieu. The Stieglitz/O'Keeffe circle included writers, philosophers and musicians as well as visual artists.

The collaboration, at once personal, social and professional, between the two was unique in the history of art.

The fact that they corresponded daily for many years while separated during the summer months is well known. The content of the letters is not. As specified in O'Keeffe's will, the letters and their contents will be revealed in the year 2020.

This collection of poetry is an attempt to imagine these letters, written by O'Keeffe in response to Stieglitz's request for 'more'.

Stieglitz photographed O'Keeffe thousands of times throughout the years, knew and loved her work probably as much as she did, and lived with her as husband and friend. Yet he felt he needed to know more about her. The letters are her response to his request.

O'Keeffe's style of writing, as evidenced by existing correspondence, is direct, economical and unconcerned with the conventions of grammar and syntax. She is quoted as saying that her paintings spoke for her; she needed to say no more. I have tried to keep O'Keeffe's voice in mind when crafting the imagined letters.

Quotes from her contemporary critics, friends and

members of the Stieglitz circle have been used to 'frame' O'Keeffe's letters; to situate them in the context of her time. The quotes provide an ongoing, objective glimpse of this extraordinary pair, their changing and enduring love, and their remarkable role in the world of Modern Art.

Alfred:

Your lens wanted everything, then.
Glass plates demanded exposure. I stood
before you, turned myself
slowly became still breath held
black box forgotten and the shutter clicks
of your heartbeat soothed shame until
it fell away and whispered
at my feet.
My small reflection showed shadows
angles and hollows unfamiliar forms suddenly squared
grey-framed in new pleasure.
My image appeared clear, steady
beneath your eye. Emerging and sharpening I
saw myself. I took on form
in your hands. You have seen everything, have
conjured the curve of lip and fixed the point
which holds the gaze. You witnessed
the birth of light.
Sly midwife.

Now you want words black
and white on paper; you want shapes
beneath the skin, equations resulting in pulse.
You want words, lines on paper, navigational charts
of my brush strokes, maps of my journey.
The cloudy glass is exhausted. Further forms wait
breathing, to be revealed.

Yes, Alfred, I will give you words now and
say the words
you need to hear.

Into all this, in 1887,
new Brooklyn Bridge, Eiffel Tower,
machine visions, black factories,
soot-skinned workers, restless expansion,
Indian Wars, I am born. Facts
I will know about later.

Sun Prairie is far from those facts. Coal dust
does not settle on my quiet quilt.
Sun does, sparkling stars;
bright flowers form
a rectangle around me.

I hear *Leatherstocking Tales* in my mother's voice,
evenings and rainy afternoons.
Green fields form patches; sewing needle shines
in Grandmother's fingers. She stitches
the pattern and border of farm life
and watches me as
I sew
hours of solitude, squares of airy spaces,
day dreams, other hours laughing
with imaginary companions in shafts of sunlight.
Loud hours of games
brothers and sisters call each others' names
and patient days spent attentive to nature's changes
of mood.
I shape these into a garment that describes
the color of my name and
the measure of my heart.

I see the seasons locked
in step,
one behind
before the other.
The certainty of the steps, the beat of the change
comforts.
The rhythm of repeated squares, familiar forms
delights.
Ice white and silence at dusk, then
soft browns and straight green rows orderly and
almost endless,
pieces of summer heat and
full gold edged in crimson assemble themselves
into a field of common patches.
I sleep beneath it,
am framed by its symmetry, sized by its dimensions.
I clutch it under my chin, wrap my bones in it.
Dark and light survey my days, mark boundaries,
indicate hours;
dawn and dusk are chimes
easy to obey.

Papa laughs
his arms filled
with acres of possibility.

Seven miles there and
seven miles back
again
with my sisters through the leafy arch
to the color house.
Shapes hid in her cupboards,
waited between pages,
napped in corners. Pigments lay pulsing
in tubes; orderly in their boxes but
ready to conspire in a riot of possibilities.
Forms fell
from her hands and
were reborn on my patient paper. My brush strokes were
obedient and mirrored her movements
for a while. I used the colors she handed me until
their names and faces became as known
as my own.
Her voice sounded in my ear until
I found a round shaped silence and
worked there. I had
so much to do.

My shoes creak on
hard waxed linoleum,
precise and measured steps
all the same
down the hall.
All the classroom doors are closed
seven ... eight
through a door window I see
the backs of many heads
bent over paperwork.
No one talks.
Another window frames a teacher speaking;
I can't hear her.
Through the next I see a flower
and the woman holding it
for the children to examine.
She turns it slowly
carefully.
A jack-in-the-pulpit.
One girl's mouth drops open,
everyone looks at the flower, then
they pick up their brushes and
each begins painting.

I am not in that room.
My fingers ache. The silk
of petals brushes my lips.

We leave today. Sun Prairie
remains behind us
as we travel east
to Virginia.
Fixed, there it will stay,
a continent away from our destination.
I take my fifteen years with me
measured out like efficient stitches
that step neatly,
hold pieces together, field greens and
ice whites worked
into a robe, bordered with shades of soil, with
the blue you see
after hours of staring at the sky.
This cloak is mine, I made it.
It will cover me in cities, confide shapes
and shades and tutor me
in the dialect of color and form.
My cloak will smell of soil and speak
of the sudden and sturdy green
plant risen, unexpectedly,
from barren grey.

This childhood garment lies light
on my shoulders. Sun Prairie,
where I learned to see and speak.

Typhoid Fever 1906

"But tell me in this strange confusion,
What is real, what delusion?
    I hear my mother speak and
    dogs yelp. I whimper
    under pounding waves of sound.
    They recede, leave me
    shaking shouts
    and whispers
    'Very grave indeed.'
Do we walk with forward faces,
Or stand and halt with baffled paces?
    My hot breath is
    breathed in again.
    Against the sheets it
    scorches my lungs,
    bloats my tongue. Hands on my chest
    burn.
All things seem to change their places,
Rocks and trees to make grimaces.
    I try to tell them but
    cracked lips don't move.
    Please catch me before I fall away and
    sink into ashy pools
    of fallen hair.
    I wait whispers of neighboring deaths are
    spoken too loudly.
And the lights in witchy row,
Twinkle more and more they blow."
    Words serve me later,
    Goethe tells part of my story.
    I remember much and move slowly,
    deliberately for almost a season.

1907
The train brings me to New York City, the
Art Students' League, West Fifty Seventh.
Manhattan soot
works its way
into my pores and between the threads
of my skirts. Noise never stops;
horses, trolleys, men move
with dizzying speed and frequency. Buildings block
the sun and wind cannot negotiate the maze
of sidewalks. Everything demands attention
which, once given, returns nothing.

Inside the school I hear the model sigh
as he wills twitching muscles still and
steadies himself for another measure of time.
Camel hair brushes stroke canvas,
palette knives push pigment together,
instructors whisper and
students nod and continue
working looking from model
to primed canvas.

One canvas a day for Mr. Chase
a new painting every day, one
on top of the other. Swift, brief
'til paint is thick
with layers of visual memory
a daily pentimento.

My fingers ache
from the desire of mastery. Only later will I learn
surrender.

Rodin drawings on display
at Gallery 291.
We are warned about them;
stupid lines and simple
splashes.
Finished work or
working sketches? Who is the fool?
Rodin or
his exhibitor?
William Merrit Chase fears questions; he almost
smells doubt
gnawing silently
at the roots of his structure.
He will never return to that gallery.
He wants to beg his students not to go.
Is there anything there? Now
they wonder.

Alfred, are you smiling
as you watch
the gallery visitors stand
before the drawings, turn
to each other in mock desperation and
move to the next framed enigma?
The struggle is what you want. The
question mark formed on the iris
gives you pleasure.

You are loud in your defence: your duty to perplex,
your mission to disturb.

(Alfred, I saw you that day
for the first time.)

If you were young, you had to find
your own way.
Yes, I said that. I tried to explain
why at twenty one
I had to leave art school,
take a job.
Father was no longer able . . .
Art school out of the question . . .
Why learn copying anyway . . .
I'll make it on my own, I'll never
never touch a brush again
if I can't do what I love.

At the agency in Chicago
I illustrate embroidery. Draft lace.
Chase's speed serves me well.
Daily deadlines, making my own way, but
my drawings are disposable here.

Then back to Williamsburg
with measles. My eyes wait in water,
don't focus enough
to work. Mother's tuberculosis stronger
than she is.
The house is always humid. Our days mold
in corners where cinder blocks join
with cold mortar. Dampness clings
to the back of our necks like
a dirty grey rag.

I will find
my own way.

Arthur said in his letters
he was going to Paris, said
it might be interesting
for me, too.
Museums, galleries and
painters are all in Europe but
he sailed without stopping
in Williamsburg.
I had a card from France.
If only he had asked.

Mrs. Willis is to take a leave of absence and
gives me the opportunity
to teach
several weeks back in Chatham
my old school.
The girls unpack eagerly
colors and charcoal; their enthusiasm
is pleasant.

I learn
not to wait
any
more.
My eyes are strong enough to see
my own way. I won't wait
for
anyone.

University of Virginia;
women were allowed
summer only
to train as teachers.
Alon Bemont teaches there and startles me
when I visit Anita's drawing class.
No plaster casts or copies
to be done.
Just new tools, fresh rules flexible enough
to use.
Arthur Dow had taught him
to see and teach
the intimate alphabet.

I finger my primer, try to shape my hands around
these new ideas.

1912 in Amarillo, Texas;
cattle drives, railways and prairies.
Fifteen thousand people bent
against the wind.
Women routinely sweep sand
down the steps and
out the door.
I walk a wooden sidewalk 'til I come to the end
of bleached boards and the beginning
of the prairie flat,
vast unbroken horizon.
Land as charged with sudden fury
as the sea; still,
then churned by wind's unseen muscle
pounding sand
into every crack.
People here are wary of weather; they fear
the fury.
I am not afraid
but breathless.

No maple leaves in Amarillo
for the children to draw.
No fruit or flowers.
The parents can't afford
to buy them.
My Dow exercises transplant badly to this arid soil.
We find stones and hard roots to work
with. 'Imagine a wall' I tell them. 'Where would
you put the door? Where would it look best?'

They lead the pony
up boards onto the table.
A child's pet animal; the hooves skid on sheets
of charcoal paper.
Juan Carlos holds the rope and we draw.
Their clumsy enthusiasm
and laughter scatter
like the missing maple leaves.

I think I taught them
to see spaces and
use them beautifully.
Ordinary things.
They studied me and saw
a new way of looking
at everyday life.

Teachers learning
to teach drawing;
my sister Anita among them.
Obedient 'Nita pleased
people; her smile softened.
Instead of sitting beside her
I stand
in front of the class, assist Alon Bemont.
'Nita's work is good but
she will never be an artist;
the fear of risk curbs her,
winds webs around her ankles.
She walks cautiously.
When I don't feel like it
I don't smile.

Bemont lends me books Kandinsky and Eddy
Cubists and Post Impressionism. Whispers
are changing to murmurs in New York.
He says I should go listen
for myself.

Aunt Ollie frees me
with her gift of money. My mother is dying;
Aunt Ollie wants me to live.

Back to New York to study
with Dow firsthand.
One needs nerve
to succeed. Yes
nerve.

N.Y.C. 1914
The Armory Show last year
Brancusi, Picasso, Matisse,
Kandinsky, Duchamp spoke the whisper
which you breathed in your gallery, Alfred.
Leaves and voices rise in the vortex and spin
slowly. Bits of paper
with important information on them swirl
in the street and settle everywhere.
Murmurs are heard even
in the quiet corners where
I paint.
One bit of paper informs me
that I can paint what I want
even if I haven't been to Europe.
One quarter million people met the work
at the Armory, listened to the hint
become the shout.

Arthur Dow is my teacher;
his love of flat forms
comforts me and tells me things
I already know.
I shed unnecessary lives and cling
to the core. I have no time
or money to waste.

Art is decadent when designers and painters lack inventive power and merely imitate nature or the creation of others.
                              Arthur Dow

Columbia University Teachers' College 1914
Kandinsky tells me
art must be moral and
the artist responsible.
My friend Anita Pollitzer tells me
of the vote, not yet grasped,
for women.
Discussion bubbles,
coffee for everyone.
Freud, socialism, O'Neill and little magazines.
We paint and study,
visit galleries; 291 of course
to see you, Alfred.
You toil and sweat
loud in your labor. You
tell me yes paintings are sold,
money earned and painters sustained.
You beg space from property owners,
nourishment from the powerful.

Pugnacious gardener you tend
with quick and awkward hands,
noisily clear away scrub that blocks
the sun. You step back and search out
new shoots. Fierce eyes turn
to anyone close,
'See it there it is'
New roots in American soil.

The artist must have something to say, for mastery over form is not the goal but rather adapting of form to its inner meaning.
                                        V. Kandinsky

1915 University of Virginia
I teach again, assist Bemont.
He still points out
markers along the path for me but now
my footsteps are less tentative.
I don't hold his hand
as tightly as
before.
I know where to look.
My subscription to 'Camera Work' reaches me
even here.
(Your whisper is heard from a distance)
I show the students photos
of modern art, read them articles
on Matisse, tell them
of the ecstasy felt
when creating.

I take long walks
with my friend Arthur McMahon
back from France,
then he's gone again.
Should a woman write the first
letter? I think I will.

I roll some watercolors, send them
to Anita in New York, wait
for her reaction.
They've made it out
of Virginia; I've sent them
flying.

August 1915
Summer term over, I have
decisions to make.
I write to Anita
'Talking of 291—and New York—
I am afraid
I'll not be there.'
I'm afraid of spending
myself in its fury, of dropping my coins
in its bright bazaar of possibilities.
I don't want to lose
my voice in the roar
of the city, or exhaust the reserves
I've saved so carefully for painting.
I won't find my pockets as empty
as my mind after a sleepless night.

The relentless green
surrounding the school
in South Carolina where I must teach
will surely speak softly enough
so I can paint undisturbed;
is surely dull enough not
to claim my time. The lack of sharp edges
reassures.

The mirrors here are dusty and
my voice sounds loud.
The school in Sumpter could be
on another planet.
Green hills hide
a dry still life.
In my room when I stop painting
long enough to listen,
what I don't hear
frightens me.
Soon I have nothing to say,
nothing.
—Anita, there's such emptiness here.
—You're strong, she writes. You'll pull through.

I walk to pass
the time
but notice now full hills green
unrolled like a sleepy blanket.
The pulse of pine forests quickens
my step. Sky seems
to fill my lungs with pure air.
I fall into the familiar,
pull old patterns around me,
measure myself to its dimensions.
Now empty hours transform themselves
to canvases
lining up for my attention.
Alone with my self,
the conversation sparkles.

Anita writes
about visits to your gallery and
life in New York.
I wonder what you would think
about my work.
I hate it now,
see obedience in every canvas,
imitation, echo. My mouth
shapes borrowed words.
My feet remember the way back
to my room, to work.

Feel of ground charcoal comforts me.
My fingers form a space
a brush fits neatly
so I continue dumb
and compliant. Need
pushes my hand across the staring page.
I work speechless until I hear
sounds riding, vowels
formed in my marrow and
wired to my fingertips;
the dispatch tapped out in my cells.
An intimate vocabulary fit
to translate my soul.
My voice audible now in the charged silence,
familiar and foreign to my ears.

I've put the caps back on the tubes
of Grumbacher pigment, flattened them evenly and
set them in a drawer.
My brushes are washed, gathered upright
in an old glass and left
to dry.

My elemental alphabet demands
simplicity. Black and white.
Charcoal and paper. Shadows and light,
dark graphs and pale, hidden skin.
I will repeat these consonants and vowels
in variations and arrangements, in
steps and flight until
we are both exhausted.

My hands ache from the work. The words
torrential now.
I roll several sheets into a tube
and send them to Anita
in New York. She takes them to you,
unrolls my soul
beneath your gaze,
your discriminating fingers.

Your voice reaches me
in Carolina.

Now you have studied them and
have seen me;
these are my words, my true
words. My drawings
are diagrams
of my days, charts of forceful currents,
maps of dreams.

Can you decipher these codes; are the cords
of your senses
tightened to this pitch?
I've stood before you, Alfred.
Do you hear my message?

"Finally, a woman on paper."

You answered, Alfred, yes.
You heard me and you know the code.
You distrust words, you say
and know about their fragile capacity.
They contain significance
so precariously.

I work all winter and spring, stop sometimes;
lift charcoal from paper
and listen patiently
for the postscript
to your letter delivered here.
I know you hear me so
I continue speaking.

There he drew out the drawings of Georgia O'Keeffe and with passion pointed out the new language in which the course of a woman's life was being unfolded.
                                        Herbert Seligmann

A letter from Texas asks me
to teach there. Says I need to learn
'methods' first.
I want to go back
to New York City to Columbia and
finish my courses. Am eager to leave
South Carolina; happy to return to friends
and movement. I leave
no notice,
move to a borrowed room
on East Sixtieth Street.

All spring I studied, learned
of Mother's death.

Alfred you unrolled my drawings and
exposed them
to crowds in your gallery.
You didn't ask me
first.
I went and saw my whispers
on the walls, bared
to many eyes. A current of cold air
made my skin tighten
even under my coat.

You weren't there that day and missed my rage.
I remained to look
at my own work.
I listened to my drawings
hum in measured spaces;
spaces once occupied by Cezannes.
I turned from one white wall,
remembered the Rodins
that once hung there and saw my charcoals
as if
they had always been there.
The right angles reassured me, the spacing
placated me. The lighting softened
my gaze.

Then I left
strangely satisfied.

I went back to 291
to confront you (do you remember?)
You stood and showed me
my drawings.

Do you realize what you've done?
The question could have been mine
too. The charcoal whisper building
to a stutter
on the walls.

Fragrance spent in the act
of blossoming
can't be contained,
you said.

June 1916.
This would be
my last summer
teaching in Virginia.

All the corners in my mother's house
are visible, the rooms empty.
I need to sleep
between classes.
My heart's angles
apparent, I move
from room
to room and forget.
I can't go outside; the sky presses
on my eyes.

Then your letters oh
Alfred, the letters find me
remind me
of other regions, other dwellings, places
I had once charted. You send me maps
for future use.

I lean on your words,
wrap myself in them, then rest
under them.

September 1916
Canyon, Texas; smaller
than Amarillo
is a tenuous toehold
on the face of the plains.
Newly civilized and has a school
where I'll teach unsupervised.
I choose materials, texts and photos.
I talk to them
about how to look
at life, how to order perception
in a beautiful way.
There are no foundations here.
I have a blueprint
and a group of eager workers.
We are busy and productive.
I almost don't notice the size
of Canyon's mind; the tight fit
of its social habit.
I can't be bothered.

Your letters and
the books you recommend
are hammers
clean and hard.

I stitch vast plains, walk in lines
straight to the horizon and
back after sunset.
Air vibrates around me,
empty planes intersect; flat sky hangs
to the floor
of the earth.
My brush is silent, charcoal vision
turns to ash.

Landscapes suddenly
suggest sienna or
sepia. Cobalt blue occurs, colors unexpectedly
introduce themselves.
I begin to practise
color consonants, shape my voice around
primary tones.
Colors dress themselves in urgency
but I have no time.

I send you watercolor notes;
cerulean blue typeface strikes wet paper.
Veils of color clothe my surroundings;
ochre margins frame
my message to you.

You hang my 'Blue Lines'
over your table and breakfast
beneath its hum.
My watercolors and charcoals hang in your gallery.
You invite visitors
to listen, then
send me reviews.
My work furnishes your days;
you live in the house
of my color.
What do you hear
with your morning cocoa?

Now when I lift my brush
at the end of the final curve,
the wet sheet rolls itself and reaches
for you.

Classes over I leave Texas
quickly; a starving animal
and arrive in New York
at 291.
I stand behind you
in silence until
you turn.

My exhibit had been photographed and
taken down
but
you hang it again;
surround me with my work, your friends and
your words which wind themselves
around my wrists, and
hide behind
my heartbeat.

Your eyes had been closed
to the camera lens, arms ached
from holding
the black metal boxes. So the cameras slept
on closet floors under piles of prints;
drowsed beside cases of negatives.
But now you want to see me
through the glass
in four inch squares, so
you begin looking
once more. You rouse the resting shutters.

In the Manhattan light I am still
again and again.
You adjust the focus and tell me
what you see. Imposed frames form small worlds,
define an instant;
fossilize time.

Back in Canyon
to teach school, I paint only
when I can.
I don't own the deed
to my days.
On sunset walks with my sister
I try to touch the evening star
with my brushes.

You send me the first photographs;
parts of my self in
black and white.
I embrace them;
recovered siblings.

This war has given my neighbors
excuses
for mean hearts and hysteria.
I find myself standing
at the meeting demanding
the man using Nietzsche
to really read the words.
My feet don't keep
the same beat; a friend
decides not to enlist and
they blame me.

Soon my mouth is dry and
my fingers won't bend
around the paintbrush.
Ice invades my joints;
a freezing wind beats
on my chest.
I feel like a trapped hare
legs pumping
in mute fury.

Into the envelope with
my images slide shades
of your solitude; greys and pale silver.
The vacant rooms of 291 have
somehow hidden themselves
in the shape of your letters.
The silence of the empty gallery
has etched itself
into the spaces
between words.

They want to close the gallery
you tell me   I could breathe
heat into it. Whisper   yes to the ember and
feed the flame.

When I look at the photos you made
I see a face I will know someday;
a self not yet formed.
The photographs flutter in my hands,
lean into the wind and
I take flight.

You wear out the most precious things you have
by letting your emotions and feelings run riot.
I wrote that to Anita when
she asked me for advice.
I should have kept the letter and
learned the lines
by heart.

Thoughts of you slip cleverly
into every minute of my day.

Your letters reach me
in Texas,
catch me as
I'm about to stumble.
I lean on your words; long
to see my image in your eyes.

Paul Strand and I arrive
in New York and find you anxious,
waiting.
Paul has done your errand and
brought me
to you,
now he moves
away.

The only sound I hear
is words on paper
as I step onto the turning wheel
of your world. East Fifty Ninth Street intersects with
the lives of so many
artists and writers; they furnish your rooms and
inhabit your time.
They are your creations now;
your cameras reap dust.

Sunlight through the panes warms me
after the late chill of Texas.
Fingers co-operative and strong.
Under the skylight my canvases appear
and turn themselves to you. They are
filled with my fingerprints;
chanting my name in three voice canon,
warm in the ready applause.

I was born in Hoboken. I am an American. Photography is my passion. The search for truth is my obsession.
                                         Alfred Stieglitz

Summer 1918
Oaklawn on Lake George,
The Stieglitz summer home.
Noise and confusion. Among children, grandchildren,
cousins, friends, guests and others I move
ill at ease; find a chair
at the family table,
the chair which still remembers
the contours of Emmeline.

You have extracted yourself only recently
from her laces and ruffles,
moved
from the shade of her parasol.

Simplicity pleases you;
bare angles and straight lines
let you breathe.
My black dresses point
to my whiteness, let color live
in the imagination.
Your fingers find lilies
under my sheets;
fragrance released.

They all leave me alone. I own
all my days here, have time
for oil colors
patient, thick, slow drying;
mid-summer greens and crimson
shape themselves
on waiting canvas. You smile at me and
color flows.

Fall 1918
You ask me what I want
most.
To paint, I say. Every day
all day
Nothing else. No one
else.
At night I need to study
the history of forms and lines,
to live in the domain of pigment and hue
in darkness
and to release the remembered colors
the next day.
I want to spend my precious currency,
time and strength
on the tight white rectangles.

My work is half the dialogue;
the mirror where I study
the suggestion of risk
imprinted on our daily life.

You tell me to step out
into the space between us,
fix the line to your eyes;
to walk the wire
and don't look
down.

Light pours in
through the skylight and
the southern window, it floods the studio
with hazy waves and
shimmers on the fittings
of my easel.

You cast no shadow, Alfred;
I never stumble over your shoes or trip
on your presence.
The finished pictures know you wait
for them; they lie quietly
in your inquisitive caress.
I meet their reflection
in your focused gaze.

Suddenly you say you must look at my work
through the glass lens;
ground perspective.
Closets are emptied, boxes upended.
The cameras sit
comfortably between us,
feet up on a worn davenport.
They pick instants from the air,
press them onto silver nitrate.

The secrets I tell you
in quiet evening hours
spin tangles between us;
our words sink
into distilled conspiracy.

My hand shakes just slightly.
I have to repeat
the brush stroke, deepen
the translucent haze of color
when I remember in daylight
our night journeys.
I retrace our steps; pieces of
our breathless climb catch
in my throat.
I feel myself fall, again,
over the edge into
shivery dark;
slow fall into
folds of silk.
I think later of the wordless descant
your tongue wrote
on my skin.
If I listen closely
the last half-note vibrates
in my brush and
exhausts itself
in fading waves of coral and crimson.
Strings now still
remember the fingers.
Colors assemble themselves on canvas
into the shape you created
inside me.
These paintings blush;
they fear others will hear
the rhythmic word
hidden in the pigment.

I am beginning to impose
rectangular frames
on daily events;
it's becoming easy to focus
on possible paintings.

Wet negatives and
rinsed prints
sleep at right angles with us;
they hang and flap
against my face
when I visit you
in the darkroom across the hall.
How many do you pull
until the negative surrenders
the perfect print?
I watch you work,
look through my lens and
see you smooth the wet images
with light and searching fingers.
Timer ticking we
embrace;
dialogue accelerates, no retreat;
charted surrender.
Released I return
to my painting,
you to the emerging images.

We hurry home
at exactly two.
The cameras stand black,
nod on thin legs;
click alert at the thought
of your footsteps.
Shutters no tighter than
sleepless eyelids.
No words are spoken;
we know our roles in this
daily dialogue.
The shape of my soul
is what you need
to seize and reflect
in positives and negatives;
grey-shaded fingerprint.
The indifferent lens magnifies
your greedy gaze.
An infinite march of seconds files slowly
into the four minute frame;
my muscles flutter with the effort
of willed stillness.
My skin is aware of the progress
of your search.
Filtered light fades;
you emerge from black-draped intensity,
eyes adjust aperture.
'Enough for today' you whisper
exhausted. 'The work of a life
time.'

You fix the lens
in my direction;
glass eye records
my creation.
You place the tutor, then
praise the bloom.
You assemble these pieces repeatedly,
discover empty spaces, unfinished images
emerging slowly.
These will need to be documented
later;
missing tiles in the black
and white montage
that is your creation.
You ask me to undress
before one of my paintings;
my work excites you;
camera is witness.
You hurry to the darkroom.

The woman forming in
acid baths and rectangular pans
is so familiar; closer than
a sister. We look in the red light reflection
at each other;
photographs more faithful
and perceptive
than any mirror.

In a part by part revelation of a woman's body, in the isolated presentation of a hand, a breast, a neck, a thigh, a leg, Stieglitz achieved the exact visual equivalent of the report of the hand or the face as it travels over the body of the beloved.
Lewis Mumford

He released forces for O'Keeffe that found expression in her paintings, and in him she released the pent-up torrents of years.
Laurie Lisle

No intelligent consideration of his later photographs can be made without mention of his relationship to O'Keeffe, for this remained the center of his life and work until his death . . . the 1917-1929 prints especially are like a rich and wonderful flowering of a man: the mature artist at the peak of his eloquence.
Doris Bry

whenever she looks at the proofs she falls in love with herself. —Or rather her Selves— There are very many.
Stieglitz to P. Strand

Although the Stieglitz portrait of O'Keeffe inevitably has its roots in the photographer and his subject, the series of prints transcends the two individuals concerned and becomes a moving symbol of the range of possibilities, life, and beauty inherent in human relationships.
Doris Bry

I have not been in Europe. I prefer to live in a room as bare as possible. I have been much photographed.
Georgia O'Keeffe

1921 Anderson Galleries NYC
'He's working again.'
That's the breeze circulating
in the close galleries;
people hurry to see
your new work. The photos of me are part
of the retrospective
1913-1921;
my body of work is exposed and delivered
to the curious and
the interested. They ask if I'm the model or
the maker of paintings.
I see only images, abstract visions of
our contingent fingerprints.
I like the way my paintings look
in the photographs.
You invite thousands
to smell the petals
in our hands.

A friend suggests I read
The Song of Songs
> 'In his longed-for shade I am seated;
> his fruit is sweet to my taste.'

I conjure the honey
and walk out of the gallery free,
filled with strength.

1921
you include me in an exhibit
of 'modern art'
Pennsylvania Academy of
the Fine Arts.

One of the organisers said "but
I don't want any goddam women
in the show."

You tell him the secret
that male and female are parts
of one being;
my work is part
of the exhibit.

Your will prevails,
insistent hands clear debris
from around shoots,
assure air,
and water.
Bloom is imminent.

Two years later you introduce my work
to the world
as you did at 291,
this time with my permission.

One hundred pieces
gathered and placed
carefully on the walls
of the Anderson Galleries.
The convocation pleases me but
I feel like I'm putting my labor
pains out in the street
to be touched and inspected
by passersby on the way
to market.

The critics have been waiting for you
to turn the page,
continue my story.
What do they mean by 'Freudian imagery'?
That has nothing to do
with my voice or
my words; my work
is my own. I'm the painter
in the photographs.
You have given me the map
and bread for the journey.

At sixty you have no interest
in babies.
You show me the poem
you wrote;
> 'The Woman Walks Homeward
> To her Little White Room
> No longer Alone
> She Carries Dawn in her Womb.'

I can walk only one path
you say.
Colors are curled
completing their term; they wait
to emerge and thrive.

Marry you Alfred?
Simplify things, you say.
Emmeline has released you;
your fingers around my wrist
tighten.

Yes, we'll marry;
I'll give you paintings
to cradle and send
on their way;
your legacy
and mine.

I fit my arms around the air
between us.

Alfred Stieglitz brought modern art to America: a great photographer, he was the first to show Picasso, Braque and Matisse in his N.Y. gallery. . . .

As their dealer, backer, leader, philosopher, and friend, Stieglitz pushed them to fame.

This memorable man and prolific talker, this evangelist, searcher and seer, sacrificed his own career as a photographer for his painters.
Mahonri Sharp Young

Stieglitz, according to W.C. Williams, was the one person able to fuse the cultural influences of Europe while at the same time maintaining, supporting, and fostering the integrity of American art.
F. Richard Thomas

He was almost as important in the history of American art as he thought he was.
Mahonri Sharp Young

They fill our rooms
with loud conversation;
ideas crackle in the hearth.
Music stitches the pieces together
into warm comfort.
Voices rise up, take on
rectangular ceiling shapes, then
sift down and curl in corners.
You feed them all,
empty your pockets
onto the table.

At the end of the evening they leave
with another layer of purpose
folded over the arm
with topcoat and scarf,
faces flushed with honest fire.
You fit a sense of belonging
on the heads like
a departing hat, a clap
on the shoulder, a call
through the opened door,
you send them off and wait
excitedly
for the return.

Your friends; artists, writers, musicians
furnish your days,
frame your evenings.
You stoke them with your ardor,
blow slowly on the embers and
warm yourself at the leaping flame.

In the back room
at the gallery
voices are raised like
flags; voices
almost heard out front
among the paintings. Fractured
planes, shattered points of view
are debated, defended.
There's no reason to add
my voice to the din.
I decide to stretch
new canvas for tomorrow;
the boys watch me work while
they consider
dreams and ego;
pause
long enough to notice
the tacks which step
in even paces along the edges.
They remark on the tight white certainty
of my frames.

I earn a space in that gallery, trade
patience and diligence
for the right to be there;
nothing to do with my place
in your bed.
I draw my silence closer;
my childhood comforter;
study my fingers for shapes, save
my breath
for the intimate dialogue
I hold daily
with color.

Do you know that Dorothy Brett
and I let ourselves into
the closed gallery
Sunday mornings, unlock
the storage room and select
favorite paintings;
arrange an exhibit;
critique with serious faces,
line and technique.
We lean and laugh.

There are women watching
me
waiting
for my next painting.
They recognise shapes that live in
all of us.

In 1920 the Nineteenth Amendment
is passed, gives voice
to womens' quiet lives.

Anita Pollitzer asks me to speak
at the Mayflower Hotel
to the assembled women.
I leave my dislike for words
at home and hear my voice
ask them to strive
and work
hard.

I hurry home to continue my own search.
You are already sleeping
warm and solid in our bed;
fierce eyes soft in darkness.
Gallery walls are waiting
for tomorrow's work.

It amuses you,
the interest in me
separate
from my work;
it sells paintings
you say.
Stories repeated solidify
into tangible outlines;
I don't recognise myself
reflected in the public eye.
Critics think they know me;
they point with brittle fingers
at the dark and private source
of my work.
They seize my paintings and
examine the abstraction.
Eyes hard with ideologies,
they measure my canvases with
Freudian rulers
satisfied
they have captured
the hidden heart.

They invade my intimate hours, expose the moment
of conception.

A friend advises me to ignore these critics.
They write about themselves;
describe
their own distortions.
You pull me close
inside your coarse woolen cloak;
raise your walking stick
to keep back the pushing crowds.

The dominion of petals and leaves is
no small one.
I wrap myself in fragrance
and sleep in the folds
of velvet and curve.
Flowers overpower me;
ambush me even
on city streets, in shop windows;
they hum as they try to pull me
into the hollows
and soft openings.
Flowers grow and thrive
on my canvas, I cannot
stop them.

I focus on the edges
of petals, and trace the statement
of stem and stamen.
I notice the shiver and
shimmer of light through leaves.
I wonder if they strain and chafe
under my close focus
as I did
when I stood before you;
ground glass eye and
you adjusted the lens.

I stand naked
before these blossoms;
I want to hide
in their secret center.

The heart of the white rose
pulses;
if only we'd listen
with intuitive ears.
Ice white and white heat
waltz on the canvas in
rhythmic complicity.

Black iris unfolds discretely;
listens to its own system
and imagines the sanctuary
of dusk.

Petals of red
poppies shudder in a sudden breeze;
its black heart asks
to be touched
by careful fingers.

Larkspur dreams of blue
sapphires and skies
right after rain;
the confident buds
bloom in profusion.

Alfred
don't let them pull off petals
one by one, expose
my secret heart.

At the corner
of Lexington and
Forty Ninth another
skyscraper raises itself
on the New York horizon;
altering man's landscape
once again.
Our rooms in the Shelton hang
in the sky;
light from the north
shimmers brilliant and
sharp on my palette.
My brushes sleep in
parallel precision like
the steel bones
of this building.
Clean right angles and
the benevolent tyranny
of geometric certainty
design my dreams
and shape my days.
Blueprint's discipline
frames my time;
I work patiently, confidently
with the authority
of the bolt's slide into measured steel.

White silk stitched
into clothing
feels cool, against my skin.
Black wool,
black cotton, cut and assembled
is warm in winter.
Why, the woman asks me,
do I always wear black?

Sparks of white illuminate
mute black;
skirts, dresses, coats, gloves
repeat the hushed message;
the close clutch
of opposites.

Peering in the mirror
I hold your negatives to the light;
see my skin dark,
and my dress light;
photographs offer proof
to the contrary.
I dress myself as I appear
inversed in your eyes;
I crystallise into light;
black lace branches
on midnight snow.

I tell the woman colors exhaust me;
the simplicity of each morning's routine
soothes me.
Black is my habit.

Taproot tries
to pierce concrete
in a blind search
for dark moisture;
it runs fingers
along edges,
feeling for fissures;
breaks in the hard fact
of asphalt.
Through my window
in the Shelton
I witness the sprout
of metal shoots;
the window frame adapts
to various angles and
I paint.

Then,
you wouldn't hang it, Alfred,
in the Seven Americans show in 1925,
do you remember?
I didn't know cities
you said.
My cityscape had to wait
until the next year.
It was the first piece sold,
twelve hundred dollars;
the price of my pride.
Then they all agreed
maybe I could paint the city after
all.
Henry MacBride said
"one of the best skyscraper paintings
I have seen anywhere."
But the city soon lost
its smile for me.

SHE PAINTED THE LILY AND GOT 25,000 AND FAME FOR DOING IT!
New York Evening Graphic 1928

What do newspapers know
about art?
Graphic type talks
about price and personality,
wonders what I look like;
an overnight success.
Truths quiet and simple meet
blocked ears.

After much deliberation,
inquiries completed,
you send my paintings
into peoples' homes
to live with them.
Not everyone wins
your approval;
you tease America
into buying its reflections
at prices that demand respect.

My calla lilies
will go to France,
mature in waxy dignity
on walls once comfortable
with European forms.
Like Lindberg last year
my lilies take wing.

I earn my own living, paint
what I want to paint.

Summers at Lake George,
relief from city rhythms;
a simple meter
of steady work,
household tasks
and garden chores
in preparation
for mid-summer's bloom.
I find childhood
pleasures again,
habits I had
lost in city's domain.
Slow cadence
pulses in my blood.
Scenes are stored,
woods remembered,
flowers filed away
for future paintings.

Your Graflex and you
follow and frame me,
squared memories.
In the darkroom
you ask me to help
spot negatives;
points of black ink
applied to white dust shadows.
We walk in comfortable concord
until late summer chill signals change;
the unavoidable fall
into Manhattan winter.

Summer 1926 Lake George N.Y.
An endless parade
of people passes
through the old house.
Feet shuffle,
voices demand,
children shriek and tumble;
colors stab at my eyes.
Duties exhaust and routines
pile on my back like
tedious bricks.

My easel wears a veil
of dust;
tubes of paint
won't surrender
their covers;
hairs split at the ends
of my brushes.
My hands clench and
open
in time with my teeth;
empty canvases stare without
blinking.

I escape
to the sea; east
to Maine.
Return to Lake George
much later when the family house is empty.

Lake George.
Hills step down
from the Adirondacks and
circle my world; they
define and tighten
my days.
The lake at the center
of a small system.
Relentless green stutters and
stands in my way;
exposes itself to me daily,
branches, leaves, stems and petals
repeat themselves.
Each new canvas looks
darkly familiar;
still lives
push at the confines of their frames and
struggle to break
my close focus.

The large and empty house
which belongs to your friends in Maine
inhabits my thoughts.

Your eyes circumscribe
my world, Alfred;
you sit just out of sight,
pretend not to wait
for my work.

Soon I stand
before
the changing faces and
vast plains
of the sea;
still liquid, then blown
into solid fury.
My lungs fill
with scrubbed air and my arms
stretch themselves
to the horizon.

Waves deliver smoothed jewels,
lay them in the sand at my feet.
Waves approach, break, and recede,
discrete and graceful.

I listen for hours,
then barely hear,
under the rumble,
the chanted answer
to desperate questions.

Lake George.
You leave me gasping
for air in dense, stuffed rooms;
in the house that has shaped itself
to generations of Stieglitz comfort.

I soak shells in seawater;
help them remember their color and cling
to wet and vibrant memory
in a teacup sea.
I paint their likeness
in my room
above the crowded din;
oils and watercolor witness
to my plight.

You won't summer at the sea and
won't build a house of our own
on the lake.
Your routine feet can't learn
new steps, you say.

You have a new darkroom
instead;
you occupy all available space.
There's no room
for me here.
Your concern has eyes;
they watch me work,
push my hand
in awkward staggers
around the canvas.
I dream fitfully
of unmeasured space.

You sit in ordered comfort,
intimate with the forms and
faces that furnish your world.
In darkened rooms you
can dance;
habit holds you by the hand.
You move in proven patterns, Alfred;
old brocade faded by
the touch of many fingers.
Burlap shadows on rugs reveal
the daily path.
While feet avoid obstacles,
unexpected wrinkles, the mind
flies elsewhere
arcs and soars,
turns familiar clouds
inside out
again and again
in ritual celebration
of their continuing significance.
You sit circled
by friends and disciples;
ideas are drawn and sharpened.
The thrust and parry
of argument
is not always bloodless, but
your passion cuts cleanly and
without malice.
You finger chord's echo,
angling ears to capture meaning
missed the note before and
you smile. Satisfied.
The familiar frees you
you say, it contains the fury.

Your words press heavy
on my forehead,
flap around
like loud and raucous geese;
scatter feathers and
raise dust.
The play of ideas tires me,
a waste of time;
attacks cut flesh
sting and burn.
A pointless exercise;
I'd rather paint.

I stumble in the maze
of your furniture.
I've emptied my room,
can see all the corners;
my brushes and colors live quietly
at the center.

Your illness stills you
suddenly;
you send out lifelines, cables to me.
I let you lean on me,
weave webs
across the space between us;
webs you want
to tighten
or cut.
I can't tell which.

Softened, I remember
why we are together;
dark eyes tell me
who I am.

Alfred, the fear and excitement
are bundled together
like an invitation to scale the face
of a sharp and bony peak.
Critics know I have the tools,
pickax and cables,
a map to the summit.
They wonder if I have
the nerve,
and desire.
They dare me;
and wait.

You and I work
intense and patient;
we sharpen the points,
check the cables for frays,
graph the map.
We smile.
You still hold the end
of the cable I walk.

Walls fall and
the box which contained me
now holds only air.
Sky inhales and
lifts me up.
Texas plains seen from schoolhouse windows
roll themselves out and under
my bed like quick carpets.
The line of horizon cuts
sharp and unbroken.
My outstretched arms take the measure
for new paintings.

I wake reluctant
to thick thoughts and footworn paths,
to layers of debris and eleven years of steps
traced around a fixed center.
The rope you hold
frays and chafes;
I focus on my feet.

Friends bring me back pieces
of travel journals imprinted with the West.
I add these to fragments
of childhood comforts and past pleasures.
I reap slippery instants,
assemble and wear them
pulled close;
they breathe slowly.

Your hands clutch tight, Alfred;
fear shines in your eyes;
eyes that still stop my heart and set color flowing.

I leave tomorrow for New Mexico.

Taos, New Mexico 1929
Here shapes finalise
their outlines, evolve
in desert heat and thin air.
A subtle and decisive turn of the lens
reveal perfect focus.
No haze hangs
between me and mountains.
Never have I seen slopes
so clearly. Sand blasts away excess;
branches, leaves and plants lean
into scouring wind. A permanent economy of line.
Heat sears thin air,
hides nothing.
I paint 'The Lawrence Tree'
from beneath the pine; top blossoms high,
surrounded by stars.

Sand shifts slowly inside me,
alters the balance;
the distance between us, Alfred,
is measured by the sand.

In the magnificent fierce morning of New Mexico one sprang awake, a new part of the soul woke up suddenly. Never is the light more pure and overweening than there arching with a royalty almost cruel over the hollow uplifting world.
D.H. Lawrence

A black Model A Ford
purchased with the currency
of my brushstrokes.
Shell and Shingle VI,
grey perceptions have given me
explorer's feet. I graph the landscape and
follow each road
to its end.
Paintings wait in dry heat.
Even here your letters find me,
remind me of white handkerchiefs.
They flutter and whimper,
limp with tears or
quickly
resemble white doves;
they glide and rise,
wings tense and just out of reach.
I shiver in a sudden flurry
of white rectangles;
they sift and settle
at my feet. Your mute emissaries
to my open spaces.

Do I cause you so much pain, Alfred?
I pack a few paintings, rugs and artifacts.
Tomorrow I return to Lake George.

Lake George 1929
Together we mend
frayed edges and worn garments;
calm hands bind months of unravelled threads
and apply the occasional patch.
We finger breaks in shared solitude, and
the fire in the wood stove is steady.
Heat releases long-tight muscles;
clenched faces loosen and assume intriguing contours.
New secrets curl on our lips;
speak of territory explored and
lessons learned.
Beethoven from your recent Victrola
counterpoints the weaver's rhythm.
Comforting habits wind themselves
around us.
I love you Alfred.

I give shape on sixteen by twenty inch canvas
to fragments of New Mexico
stored in my pockets
like smooth stones.
They bloom before me, flame
orange and red in New York November;
then back to the city where
rumors of collapse run
like rats along the bottom edge of buildings.
Ten million people unemployed.

At 509 Madison Avenue you open An American Place;
surround me again with my work,
smile slyly at me from the corner.

April 1930 Lake George
Jack-in-the-pulpits hide
just behind
newly green trees. Jack in the center unseen until
viewed from the proper angle.
Stiff dignity
rises from sheltering petals.
Footsteps fall in memory
tumble down a polished hall
to the door-window which frames
a jack-in-the-pulpit
turned this way
and that;
watched by eager eyes.
Now I mix pigment slowly, colors bound in oil;
fix the image
on the retina
and turn to transplant
bloom on canvas.

But soon again there is nothing here to paint, nothing.
Your eyes a blank mirror.
Damp repeated green molds and thickens;
greedily sucks in air,
a photosynthesis gone awry.

In my room, watched by unblinking easel I focus
on distant points.
If I'm very still I can hear
the flat and vast hum
of empty acres.
I can conjure the air-filled ecstasy;
the sky draped feast.

I will leave again, Alfred
Again and

again I rise
from close and sheltering hands;
I have no choice.

I have wanted to paint the desert and I haven't known how. The bones seem to cut sharply to the center of something that is keenly alive on the desert even tho' it is vast and empty and untouchable—and knows no kindness with all its beauty.
                                        Georgia O'Keeffe

Bones emerge
from acres of sand; pieces of tooth
that work their way out
through the gum,
days after the dentist.
Bones blasted by sand, wind-driven sculpture
now indestructible.

Bones wait
in an ochre sea
confident of their place in the code.
They rehearse; limber voices;
anticipate the arid chorus.
I rush to gather them,
examine each and listen.
Skulls and thighbones, fragments of pelvis
frame pieces of sky when I hold them up.
Animal bones, hard bleached survivors, they sing
in the desert.
They are like your clouds, Alfred,
equivalents of the desert.

I paint them daily,
pack bones to ship back East
to furnish my exile.

Framed by my Ford I
look back at you
from the photographs.
Evident in my eyes is
the sound of the engine running.
Sparks of sun glance
hammered on the hood like a fist
forging new forms.
Hard polished chrome work
shines in the Indian silver bracelet
brought back from New Mexico
to circle my wrist.
You record my departures, count
the road signs, indicators of absence;
note my arrivals
in strife's notebook. Smudged pages,
thumbed corners,
unsteady columns of figures
testify in the court
of husband and wife.

In late spring you shiver, dress
in layers of clothing;
hurry to close
the door behind me as I drive West
with all the windows open.
In the rear view mirror you recede,
a small dark form draped
in mourning crepe.
Paintings as numerous
as grains of sand glitter
before me, mark the miles
I've travelled.

There has been one who has stood by me through it all—a girl from Texas.

A. Stieglitz

My feeling about life is a curious kind of triumphant feeling about—seeing it bleak—knowing it so and walking into it fearlessly because one has no choice—enjoying one's consciousness.

G. O'Keeffe

1931 near Taos
I rise sleepless just hours after midnight,
climb onto the flat adobe roof,
lie and wait for dawn
to cover me with cool pressed sheets and
bound borders.
The bed of desert is immense and empty;
your even breathing is inaudible, Alfred.
I live in rooms of routine;
paintings tick slowly
in hours of solitude.
I want to pull the edges of canvas
around me,
loosen in its measured comfort, turn
back the corners of white rectangles and
lie with you.
As I wrote to Beck Strand,
there is something about being with Stieglitz
that makes up for landscape.

I return early to Lake George this year, carrying
the desert shaped hollow
in my arms.

You flee to the city,
captive to other interests
as you once were
to me. Our dance continues;
advance and
retreat, pull
and push, psalm and silence.
Our feet trace ancient,
tentative patterns.

A trip to the sea crosses
in Gaspé.
They wait patient, arms reach lightly out
for the sailors.
White French-Canadian crosses rise
and conspire with gulls;
slim fingers touch sea mist,
a world away from massive black
Penitent crosses pressing heavy;
a wooden vise
on the landscape of New Mexico.
I bring back paintings,
worn barns and crosses, farmhouses
and cold forests
to add to the bones and sand,
canyons and cliffs,
sun colors and arroyas.
I tie them in strings of need and
lay them in your lap
Alfred
my heart's parcel.
Your eyes catalogue swiftly,
smile briefly and then
speak to someone over my shoulder.

Donald Deskey was the designer of the Music Hall interiors. His intent was to make the theatre into a public gallery of contemporary art, decorated by first-rate modern artists. In the spring of '32 he approached O'Keeffe, offering her fifteen hundred dollars to paint a mural. . . . She agreed to Deskey's proposal, in spite of the small fee.
R. Robinson

Stieglitz had always glorified in O'Keeffe's work. He had seen it, quite properly, as the expression of herself, that core of identity which he honored and cherished. His adamant and violent rejection of O'Keeffe's plan, and his hostility toward her projected work, was a violent rejection of herself.
R. Robinson

He felt she was publicly betraying him as an agent and as a husband, as a commercial and philosophical partner.
R. Robinson

The confrontation was part of a continuing dynamic. O'Keeffe was acting as an independent person and artist at some cost to the marriage. Her cool exclusion of Stieglitz from the Music Hall negotiations made a statement that he found subversive and threatening. The case for Stieglitz as the betrayed husband was strong, defensible, and easily articulated. The unspoken subtext, of course, was Stieglitz's public betrayal of O'Keeffe with Dorothy Norman.
R. Robinson

Canvas peels;
sly and silent, it
detaches itself
from wet plaster as I watch,
hands full of brushes and
colors ready.
Cloth edges curl and roll,
resist mending fingers;
nervous workmen reassure,
smile,
glance as
upper corners surrender
to gravity.
The ceiling wrinkles and sags;
thin skin falls
away from bone before our upturned faces.
Canvas collapses around me;
the plaster will never dry.
Everyone watches
my face.
They are uneasy
witnesses to the conspiracy
of refusal.

Dreams slice my nights
into damp slivers, fears
that pulse in my chest.
Frames warp and snap,
tacks scatter,
canvas unweaves itself and molds
in heaps of tangled fiber;
others sidestep my brush.
Pigments pull apart on a shaky palette,
metal filings to magnets.
Colors drain and gasp, shapes surrender
their borders.
My fingers chase drops
of mercury
on twisted planes.
White pillowslip calibrates sleep's fever;
I wake to icy wilderness.

You hand me camellia blossoms white
as the sheets,
set lilies on the bedstand to guard me
while you're gone.
You press cold linens of regret
on my forehead and circle
my sickbed
with steps of worry. You arrange my paintings
Alfred, a retrospective mask
over the empty spaces.
Your hands tend
and till as they did
years ago
but
they can't reach me
now.
I'm down too far below the surface;
white-green shoots wait
breathing, unable to move
towards light.

You seem to have given me a strangely beautiful feeling of balance that makes the days seem very precious to me—I seem to have come to life in such a quiet surprising fashion—as tho I am not sick any more. Everything in me begins to move and I feel like a really positive thing again.

Maybe the quality that we have in common is relentlessness— maybe the thing that attracts me to you separates me from you.

I want you—sometimes terribly—but I like it that I am quite apart from you like the snow on the mountain.

I do know that the demands of my plot of earth are relentless if anything is to grow in it—worthy of its quality . . . If the past year or two or three has taught me anything it is that my plot of earth must be tended with absurd care—By myself first— and if second by someone else it must be with absolute trust— . . . It seems it would be very difficult for me to live if it were wrecked again just now.

When I felt well, though, I had a sense of power. I always had it.

It will undoubtedly take quite a period of fumbling before I start on a new path, but I'm started, and seem to settle down to it every day as tho it is the only thing to do. There were talks that seemed almost to kill me—and surprisingly strong sweet beautiful things seemed to come from them. The days with Alfred were very dear to me in a way—it was very difficult to leave him but I knew I could not stay.
O'Keeffe to Jean Toomer
a writer and member of the
Black renaissance movement.

Sunset's veil falls on desert colors,
charcoals, red and yellow ochres,
buff-colored sand and sage.
Grey green trees, piñon pines briefly
wear muted tones, then
full bright again beneath sheer
billowing curtains of light and dark;
a shifting palette.
Every window frames
a deliberate composition.

I take off my dress and lie
on the hot sand when
no one is near; I
try to press myself
into it. I hold the sand
in my hands,
use a mortar and pestle to grind soil and
then mix it with linseed oil
and try to paint with it.
Colors here have settled
behind by eyes;
wind has driven them
through my skin, into
my joints;
brushstrokes as close
as my lips forming sound.

Hills sleep
around my adobe home;
umbers, greys and shadowy blues lie
lightly on waves of sand. They seem
to draw close then
fall away.
Silence breathes evenly in
silken dominion; a vast sea of stillness.

I'll be with you again soon
Alfred.
I imagine you
reading my letters
in the study at
the farmhouse. Your day's traces
echo even here.
I move with care through hours
confident now
that the chords of my pictures
vibrate
in your inner ear.

Ram's Head with Hollyhock 1935
Ranchos Church 1930
Summer Days 1936
From the Faraway Nearby 1937

. . . ripe with beauty, touched by grace, buoyant with vision, sure in execution, clear as to character.
Ralph Flint,
Art News

The directness of transcription from feeling to symbol gives the best of the canvases a special and distinguished place of their own to which few contemporaries, however talented, have access. These pictures are not derivations, they are sources.
Lewis Mumford,
The New Yorker

1938
The last photographs
at Lake George
fall like fruit
into my hands.
I sit framed by
late-summer gardens; a deliberate instant
crafted from our days.
Apples fallen from the tree
near the southeast corner
of the farmhouse
multiply in my hands like promises
made that spring years ago
when you held the ladder and
I climbed, and with the saw
shaped the tree, left only
fruit bearing branches. The slow-growing
earth guided branches; they bend now
heavy with fruit, redeemed
by ruthless pruning.

Your hands cannot hold
the heavy cameras any
longer;
no lens defines us now.
Your eyes blink,
adjust to new light.

1938
Alfred,
the new apartment
has more space and
light;
the balcony looks over
the East River.
Sky seems to lean in
through northern windows.
There's room for the housekeeper;
I've had the phone installed.
I wish I could be there all
the time
to settle you in and
sit next to you in the evening.
Sometimes when I picture my heart
stones appear on my canvas.

I followed your map to New Mexico,
crated three new paintings today;
will ship them East tomorrow morning
to whisper in your ears
descriptions of my journey.
I wish you could be here, the same sky
has wrapped us both in its arms.

I don't believe she ever did anything contrary to her own inner feeling.

A. Stieglitz

I believe it was the work that kept me with him—tho I loved him as a human being . . . I put up with what seemed to me a good deal of contradictory nonsense because of what seemed clear and bright and wonderful.

G. O'Keeffe

The paintings tick here in
bountiful hours,
practised days.
Wind-driven sand scours,
leaves only bone.
Dawn quickens black cliffs and
sparks ash white sand formations;
daily I witness light
and describe it to my canvas.
Brushes retrace shapes
imprinted on the eyes. I record images;
the Sangre de Cristo mountains glisten
miles away and in my studio. The Black Place and
the White Place tangle in shadows;
meet on my easel.
I walk on ground
sacred to the Navajo;
part of their rituals.
Reasons for the consecration
slumber in cracks, deep
in centuries of silence.

The Art Institute of Chicago
assembles a picture of my work.
I send them messages received
from the fissures pried into mountains;
cliffs split,
watered by secret springs.

Pelvis with Moon 1943
Pelvis Series, Red with Yellow 1945
Two Jimson Weeds 1938

It is my private mountain. It belongs to me. God told me if I painted it enough, I could have it.

G. O'Keeffe

Cebolla Church 1945
Black Cross, New Mexico 1929
Black Place III 1944
The Grey Hills 1942

1945
I watch the world
through holes in desert bones;
sky, mountains, fabric flowers and the moon
appear in my telescope
of pelvic bones. Animal bones I have found.
I fix images
one by one
in lasting frames.
My artifacts have visited death
and returned to sandy bloom.
Sky seen through this aperture
is a fragile blue sapphire.

Gas is rationed, butter too.
Los Alamos is forty miles away but
sifts like black ash
into shop counter conversations.
The world beyond me
is visiting death.

I scrape my palette clean,
take my pigment from new tubes and
wash my brushes twice.
The weight of my task sleeps like lead
behind my ribs.
I paint a flaming red sky seen
through gold bones.
Maria turns on the radio;
flesh is falling off
burning bones
somewhere in Japan.

Arrived today in Abiquiu;
your letter was waiting
for me.
I'm sad to hear
An American Place
is so quiet now;
your garden plot, medium
for so many, empty now.
Sturdy bold shoots
shake soil from roots
and bloom elsewhere,
far from the gardener's hands.
I know you're tired, Alfred, but
don't cultivate bitter fruit now.

Woven into each of my primed canvases
are minute squares that frame your likeness;
strong white threads that carry color
like cabled dispatches.
We each hold one end, bound
in this continuing dialogue.

Incredible, just incredible.

A. Stieglitz

O'Keeffe is beautiful. She is beautiful in every respect.

A. Stieglitz

I see Alfred as an old man that I am very fond of—growing older—so that it sometimes shocks and startles me when he looks particularly pale and tired... Aside from my fondness for him personally I feel that he has been very important to something that has made my world for me—I like it that I can make him feel that I have hold of his hand to steady him as he goes on.

G. O'Keeffe

I watched it happen;
you ceased
breathing today
Alfred.
The last image fixed
on clouded eyes
is mine.
The curve of cornea
refracts
light and shadow;
dark rectangles on
hospital bleached sheets;
pale hands holding
the dark sleeve
of my dress.

Earlier
newsprint left witness
on white walls
as you fell;
reviews of my exhibit,
typeface on rag paper
clutched in your hand.

Hours of searching
noisy Manhattan
yields a coffin
planed
by careful hands.
Straight and silent pine boards
join flawlessly;
right angles and corners.
I tear out
sugar and spun satin and
lay white linen
coarse and unbleached

in its place.
I smoothe wrinkles
with slow fingers;
make clean corners and
cool folds.
Afterwards
they hand me
your
ashes.

The black bird
on my canvas
stitches earth
to sky.
It carries the horizon
on slim wings;
rises
in heavy flight;
holds air
in hollow wing bones.
It flies away for
ever,
leaves me
a dark space
that flows out
from the slow beat
of ebony feathers.
My paintbrush explores
the frontiers
of your absence.

A sudden snow whitens
red hills; pearls lie quiet
beneath sooty shadow;
paper waits
for the charcoal word;

the outline of your ashes
on ice.

Clusters of crystals
form
where light hits hardest;
silver emulsion
pulses dense
and dark.
Focused light filters through and
leaves a white aperture
on light-sensitive paper.
You shone on me
without blinking;
now I cast
a permanent image.

Boxes and boxes of prints,
plates and negatives
are roused
from closet sleep.
Fingerprints
on time's white pages;
they identify the man.
A black and white diary
of days;
this description of light
spoken by a life
time.
A catalogue of instants
that speaks
your name.

I assemble my image
from the deck of negatives
dealt again and again.

I hold them up
to the light;
search for sharp edges and
grey-shaded dreams;
look into the mirror
of my eyes.

You wanted everything then
Alfred;
insistent fingers
soothed and aroused.
I made myself transparent and
shattered your white light
into a profusion
of blossoms;
a brilliant shower
of forms and colors.

I will whisper
words to you;
fluent brushes and
ready canvas
continue
the intimate dialogue.

Although *The Intimate Alphabet* is fiction, it is shaped and informed by the following texts. I am grateful to the authors.

Bry, Doris. *Alfred Stieglitz Photographer.* Boston: Museum of Fine Arts Press, 1965.

Castro, Jan Garden. *The Art and Life of Georgia O'Keeffe.* New York: Crown Publishing, Inc., 1985.

Cowart, Jack and Juan Hamilton. *Georgia O'Keeffe Art and Letters.* Washington: National Gallery of Art, 1987.

Frank, Waldo, ed. *America and Alfred Stieglitz: A Collective Portrait.* Doubleday, Doran and Company, 1934.

Lisle, Laurie. *Portrait of an Artist.* New York: Washington Square Press, 1980.

Messinger, Lisa Mintz. *Georgia O'Keeffe.* Thames and Hudson, 1988.

Norman, Dorothy. *An American Seer.* New York: Random House, 1960.

O'Keeffe, Georgia. *Georgia O'Keeffe.* New York: The Viking Press, 1976.

Pollitzer, Anita. *A Woman on Paper.* New York: Simon and Shuster, 1988.

Robinson, Roxana. *Georgia O'Keeffe: A Life.* New York: Harper and Row Publishers, 1989.

Thomas, F. Richard. *Literary Admirers of Alfred Stieglitz.* Carbondale: Southern Illinois University Press, 1983.

Wilder, Mitchell, ed. *Georgia O'Keeffe. An Exhibition of the Work of the Artist.* New York: Clark and Way Inc., 1966.

Young, Mahonri Sharp. *American Moderns.* New York: Watson Guptill Publishing, 1974.